TONE

THE EXPLOIT OF

EBB ELLIS,

FOR THE RULES OF FOOTBALL

N HIS TIME

S ARMS AND RAN WITH IT

STINCTIVE FEATURE OF

Y GAME.

323

RUGBY
the golden age

RU

the golden

GBY
age

John Tennant

CASSELL
ILLUSTRATED

First published in 2005 by
Cassell Illustrated
a division of Octopus Publishing Group Limited
2-4 Heron Quays
London E14 4JP

Designed by John Tennant

A CIP catalogue record for this book is
available from the British Library.

ISBN 1-84403-2906
EAN 9781844032907

Printed in China.

FOREWORD

'It frequently happens... that the operator himself discovers on examination, perhaps long afterwards, that he had depicted many things he had no notion of at the time'
WILLIAM HENRY FOX TALBOT

'Rugby football is a game for gentlemen in all classes, but for no bad sportsman in any class'
BARBARIAN MOTTO

THEY ARE LINKED BY COMMON ROOTS, yet the two codes of rugby football have resolutely followed their separate paths for more than a century – ever since being torn apart at a meeting at the George Hotel, Huddersfield, in 1895. This bitter divorce – over 'broken-time' payments to players from Northern clubs – has been played out in public, with its full share of jealousy and distrust, accompanied by claims of superiority and inferiority, from both sides.

In spite of this history, the two codes maintain the same notion of the inclusive nature of 'the club'. Supporters invariably feel part of proceedings in a way that few sports can match, and are entertained by players still blessed with a genuine love for their sport. It is these enduring qualities that truly unite both games.

There is both Union and League in this book and it would be a fine piece of sophistry to separate them into the clichéd 'soft, middle-class Southerner' and 'gritty Northerner' pigeon-holes rather than celebrate the sense of togetherness, passion and enjoyment that both codes possess.

This book of photographs, like my books on football and motor racing that came before it, should be prefaced with an explanation of the approach taken in its research and assembly.

Rugby The Golden Age is all about sport and photography but not about 'sport photography' in its literal sense, and certainly not in its current incarnation of tight long-lens action shots with the protagonist filling the frame and the background thrown out of focus. I want to show there is more to photographing sport than 'Chest Breaks Tape', 'Man With Fish' and 'Ball Bursts Net' pictures and that those photographs often capture little atmosphere and are, ultimately, peripheral, even superficial.

The images in this book represent a golden age of the photography of rugby; photographs that are about the detail and not fixated on achievement. The current preoccupation with winners suggests that sometimes the best pictures might not be considered for anthologies, although people tend to assume they have been. The best photographs – strange, beautiful or comical – are never mere anecdotal illustrations of important events, but images in their own right. And sometimes these images seem to select themselves, as if the collection has a life of its own, insisting on the inclusion of one photograph and denying another.

A considerable number of the images in this book were made when clumsy, large-format equipment dictated a more measured approach; a process of composition and consideration, rather than a frenzied, motor-driven response. They reflect a way of looking that seems to have disappeared from the pages of our newspapers and magazines.

In the early days of newspaper photography there was no such thing as a specialist sports photographer. They were expected to be able to tackle anything, in the words of the old Beaverbrook Daily Express mantra, 'from a sausage to a submarine'. The quality of the images produced during this period actually seems to benefit from this wider perspective.

Today's press photographers, whatever their speciality, may be required to cover many stories in a day, only possible due to of all kinds of advances in everyday life, not least in the areas of digital technology and travel. Many of the images in this book come from a time when international journeys were by sea and it took six weeks to travel from England to Australia or New Zealand.

Wherever it has been possible, the photographs are attributed, although most of the old picture agencies operated on the basis that their names, not those of individual photographers, were credited. As a result, the 'Unknown Photographer' is well represented.

Whilst the book is not bound to a succession of winners it is, most definitely, a slave to research: the hunt for the unusual, unpublished and unknown in archives and libraries. Sometimes this research consisted of sifting through dusty prints or poring over fragile glass negatives, shelved and forgotten for fifty years or more. However grimy this process might be, it remains more fun and potentially more rewarding than the ubiquitous electronic browser.

Many of these archive prints are only sketchily captioned (sometimes, not at all) and I am deeply grateful for the unstinting help that Howard Evans and Robert Gate have given me in identifying players, grounds and matches.

Rugby The Golden Age is neither a narrative nor a comprehensive history – it is an Aladdin's cave. I have not worked from a list of 'must-have' players. Instead I have let the power of each image claim its place. You will find no mud-caked, primordial Fran Cotton, no topless Erica Rowe, and no 'Great Tries'. But there is a lot of accidental and unintentional beauty, maybe a tiny detail on the periphery of whatever was intended to be the focus of attention, that is sufficient to mark out a picture and transform the potentially mundane into something extraordinary and memorable. JOHN TENNANT

INTRODUCTION by JPR Williams

HE GAME OF RUGBY was allegedly born in 1823 when William Webb Ellis picked up the ball during a football match at Rugby School in England. Up until that time, the ball was there to be kicked, not handled. Webb Ellis caused a rumpus by this act but it led to the foundation of rugby as we know it today. The game has always been very robust and the initial instigators of rugby in England started to play with great enthusiasm in the mid-1800's. Guy's Hospital and Blackheath were two of the inaugural clubs, the growth of which eventually led to the formation of the National Unions – England in 1872, Scotland in 1873, Ireland in 1875 and Wales in 1878. Popularity in Britain was soon followed by support for the game in Australia, New Zealand, South Africa, France and Italy, and rugby now prospers as an internationally popular game.

In England, rugby started out as a 'middle class' game, played in public schools, but this quickly caused difficulties in Lancashire, Yorkshire and Cumbria. These were mining areas in the north of the country where life was hard and money not abundant. Unsurprisingly, the players wanted some recompense for missing mining shifts while playing for their rugby team. A conflict arose as the game of the time was played strictly on an amateur basis, with no payment allowed for playing a match. In 1895, this dispute led to the formation of a professional rugby league, based in the North. Over the next thirty years, this league developed into a separate game with its own code of play, distinct from Rugby Union, and in 1922 it officially became known as the Rugby Football League. Despite efforts from South Wales and London, the North of England is still the home of Rugby League in Britain.

In 1995 Rugby Union also became professional. Ironically, since then, the game has become increasingly popular – especially in Britain as England have had a very successful era that culminated in victory in the 2003 World Cup in Australia. Both Union and League are great games and since Union went professional, there have been tremendous new links between the coaches and players of both codes. Coaching and skills are swapped between the two as never before.

The early days of rugby were all about enjoyment, with players relying on the good will of groundsmen, ladies making tea, and 'rub-a-dub' men. This is a common denominator between Union and League, and there are still many volunteers behind the scenes, making certain that, whatever happens in the result, both teams and sets of supporters enjoy themselves. The other unsung heroes in rugby are the referees. Whatever the referee does, he will be criticised by one side or the other. In rugby, the final decision lies with the referee and any arguments from a player will result in an immediate penalty. The referee won't put up with continual infringements of the rules despite warnings, and players must accept his decision. I feel this is an excellent situation and perhaps one that soccer could learn from!

Rugby has survived over 130 years of recognised play. There is no longer friction between Union and League and there is no doubt the two games are getting increasingly close in terms of fitness, skill and play. All sizes of players are catered for in both

codes – scrum halves cannot be tall and prop forwards still have to be tough.

The photographs in this book reach to the heart of rugby – a hard game, played by hard men. Not for them the pretence of a foul against them – no, grin and bear it! It has been said that rugby is a thug's game played by gentlemen but soccer is a gentleman's game played by thugs! Although it's hard to believe it now, rugby in its early days attracted a lot of very intelligent people. I have played many sports and I can honestly say that rugby is the most enjoyable of the lot. It encapsulates skills, strength, intelligence, team spirit and offers the physical contact that a lot of people like.

John Tennant has produced excellent books on football and motor racing with wonderful photographs and I can only endorse his work on rugby. These images really do capture the spirit of rugby from 1900–1980, with the players caught on camera both on and off the field. Spectators and helpers behind the scenes also represent our own enjoyment of the game from the sidelines. The game can only continue to improve on and off the field and perhaps one day Union and League will combine to form one game of rugby. JPR WILLIAMS

St. Mary's versus
Guy's in the
Hospital Cup Final.
March 1938.
Photograph by
A. Hudson

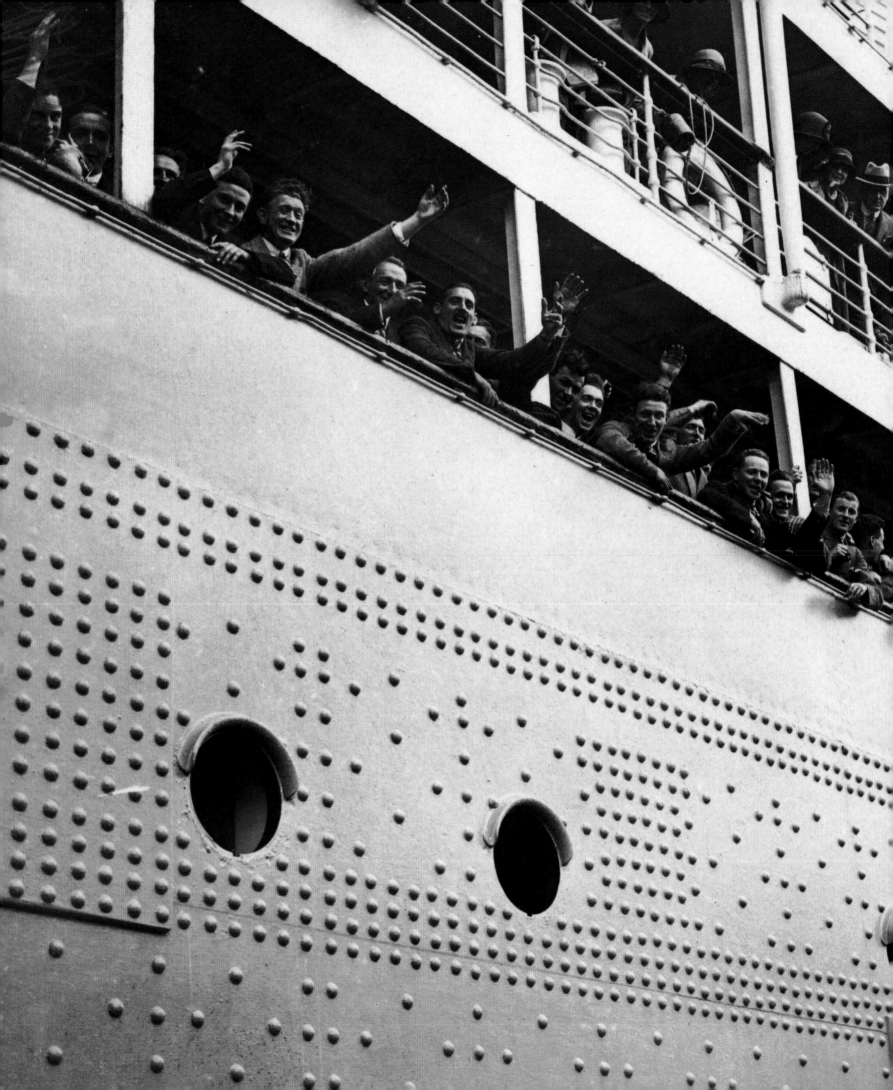

The British Isles Rugby Union touring team leave Southampton for South Africa, on board the 'Edinburgh Castle'. June 1924. Photograph by E. Bacon

British soldiers interred at Groningen camp by the Dutch, who remain a neutral state. Circa 1916. Photographer not known

William Ellis School in Kentish Town has taken up rugby due to the lack of qualified football coaches. November 1957. Photographer not known

Leeds stand-off, Lewis Jones coaches pupils at Castleton School. Circa 1960. Photographer not known

Australia versus London
Australians at Queen's Club,
Kensington. September 1916.
Photograph by W.G. Phillips

Australian Geoff Burke, loose forward
for Leigh RLFC, with Mr. G. Sims,
the club secretary. December 1949.
Photograph by John Chillingworth

20

Irish supporters in London for the match against England. February 1937. Photographer not known

Scottish supporters in Leicester Square before the match against England. March 1936. Photograph by E. Dean

Esher RFC hold a regular Thursday evening inquest on their previous game.
December 1952. Photograph by Peter Waugh

Opposite: Albert Pepperell discusses Workington's recent match against Leeds with locals at the New Crown.
November 1950. Photograph by Jack Esten

Twickenham crowd before
England play Scotland.
March 1938.
Photographer not known

New Zealand winger Ron Jarden at an All Blacks training session during their European tour.
February 1954. Photograph by Raymond Kleboe

Opposite: Warlingham versus Old Haileyburians. October 1951. Photograph by Henri Cartier-Bresson

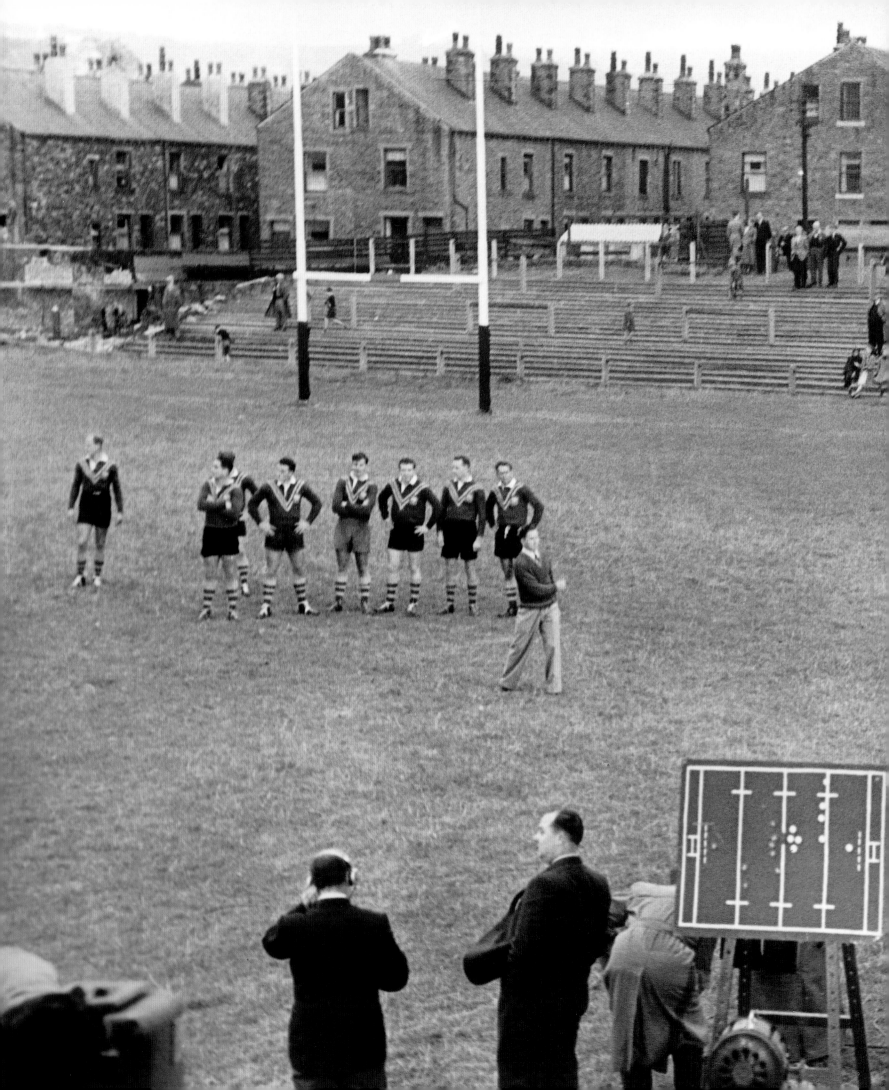

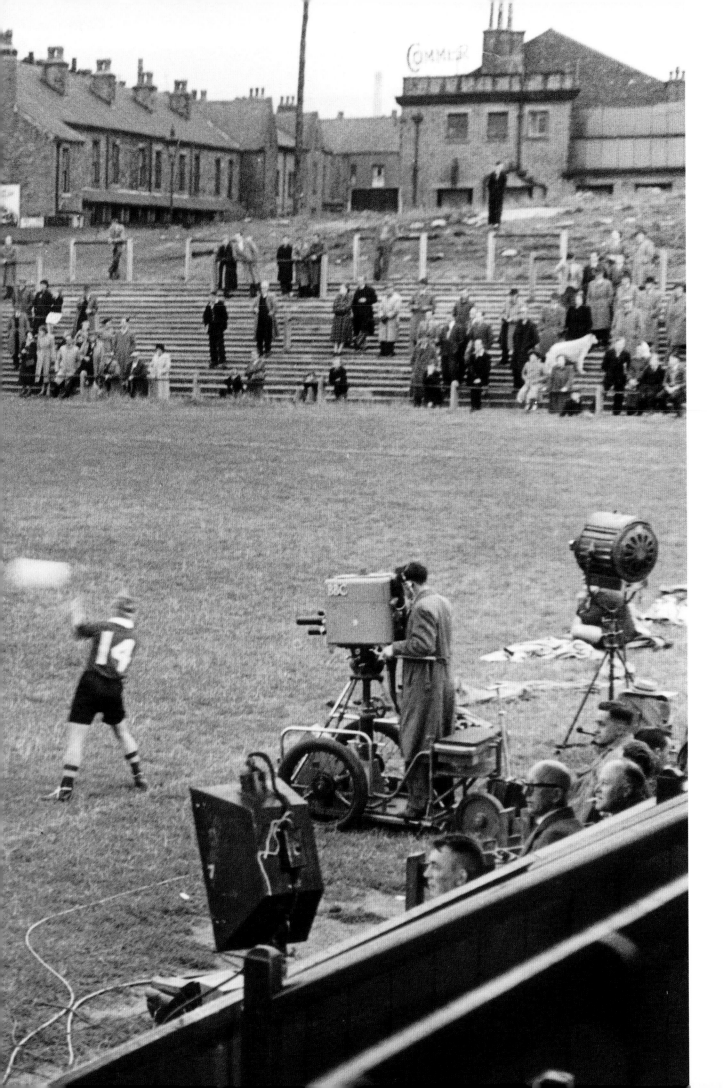

The Australian
Rugby League squad
prepare for the
Ashes series at
Lawkholme Lane,
Keighley.
September 1952.
Photograph by
J. Simmons

The Welsh team visit the Forth Bridge. January 1934. Photograph by D. Thomas

The Welsh team outside their hotel in Paris. April 1930. Photographer not known

Whitehaven's Billy Banks, who is also a taxi driver, and Australian player Kevin Brasch use the running board to get changed. November 1957. Photographer not known

Opposite: St. Mary's players, known as the 'Belles of St Mary's', recover after their game against Riverstone. New South Wales. May 1956. Photograph by Dennis Rowe

Above and opposite: Mill Hill School pupils practise their tackling. February 1937. Photographer not known

The All Blacks 'Invincibles'
with their team mascot before
the match against England at
Twickenham. January 1925.

The new section of the Chertsey Road will stop the two-mile long traffic jam going to Twickenham. December 1933. Photographer not known

Some cars have to be parked almost a mile away from Twickenham when England play France. February 1957. Photographer not known

The Kiwis after their Rugby League Test Match against England at Warrington Oval.
December 1951. Photograph by Ronald Startup

Opposite: An England player receives treatment during the Rugby League Test Match
versus Australia at Sydney Cricket Ground. January 1950. Photographer not known

Esher Rugby Club match. December 1952.
Photograph by Peter Waugh

Opposite: B.H. Black converts a try for England against Scotland
at Murrayfield. March 1931. Photographer not known

**British Lions relax on the
Tasman Glacier, New Zealand. August 1930.**
Photographer not known

Above and opposite: Salford players prepare for the Rugby League Cup Final against Barrow. May 1938. Photographer not known

Floodlit practice, location not known.
October 1933.
Photograph by R. Wesley

Practice at Stowe School. December 1946. Photograph by Francis Reiss

Opposite: In front of Cardiff City Hall. May 1935. Photographer not known

Bert the boiler man at Wigan RLFC.
December 1950. Photograph by Charles Hewitt

Opposite: The victorious Widnes team after their
Rugby League Cup Final against Hull Kingston Rovers
at Wembley. May 1964. Photographer not known

Coach and players discuss tactics. Location not known. Circa 1935. Photographer not known

Welsh international Vivian Jenkins with players at Dover College. August 1933. Photograph by R. Wesley

Scotland versus Ireland at Murrayfield. March 1955. Photograph by Malcolm Dunbar

Supporters in the Mall before the Rugby League Cup Final between Salford and Barrow. May 1938. Photographer not known

Opposite: In Trafalgar Square before Huddersfield play Warrington in the Rugby League Cup Final. May 1933. Photograph by J.A. Hampton

**Wembley staff prepare
for the Rugby League
Cup Final. May 1933.**
Photographer not known

Schoolboys practise scrummaging at Eltham College, London. November 1943. Photograph by Harry Todd

Ireland versus England, Lansdowne Road, Dublin.
March 1951. Photograph by William Vanderson

Opposite: Fans are locked out at Twickenham before England play Wales.
January 1929. Photographer not known

Wigan forward Ted Slevin earns
£7 a week as a furniture 'humper'.
December 1950.
Photograph by Charles Hewitt

John Snagge and Teddy Wakelam commentate on England versus South Africa using a grid reference pattern – published in the Radio Times – which enables listeners to locate the area of play. The system is said to be the origin of the expression 'back to square one'. January 1932. Photographer not known

Opposite: BBC hut and van at Twickenham for the match between England and Wales. This will be the first live radio commentary. January 1927. Photographer not known

England practise at St George's
College, Weybridge. February 1964.

London University students organise a Men versus Women match. March 1963. Photographer not known

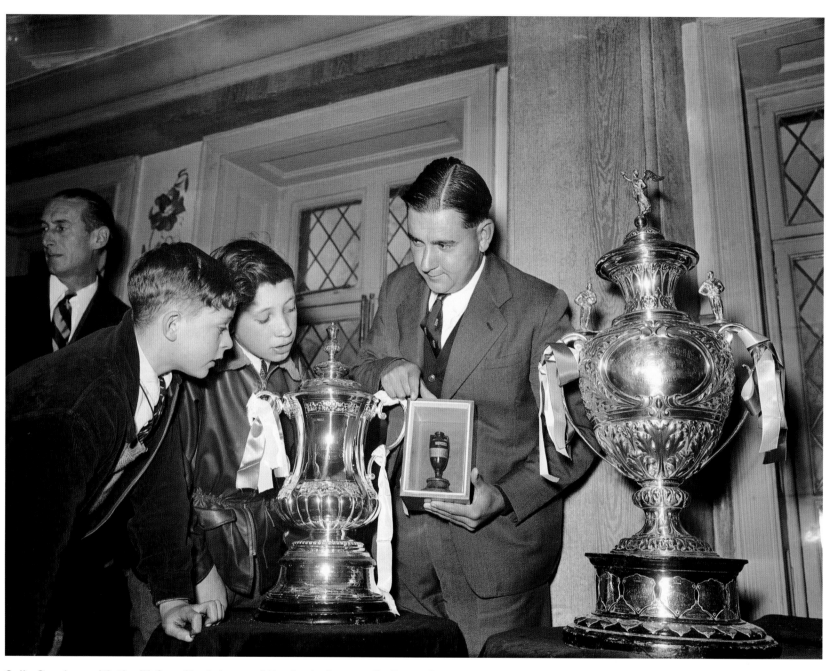

Colin Cowdrey with the FA Cup, the Ashes and the Rugby League Challenge Cup at the Sporting Trophies Exhibition at the Café Anglais, London. April 1956. Photographer not known

The Rugby League World Cup at the Sporting Trophies Exhibition at Cheeseman's department store, Lewisham. January 1955. Photograph by S. Martin

Workmen at Cardiff Arms Park.
May 1958. Photograph by Maeers

Opposite: Cardiff Arms Park.
December 1960. Photograph by Edward Miller

Gus Risman holds the Rugby
League Challenge Cup after
Salford beat Barrow at Wembley.
May 1938. Photograph by Dennis Oulds

Widnes players Hugh McDowell and Walter Bradley. May 1937. Photographer not known

Local game, location not known. Circa 1960. Photographer not known

Anti-apartheid demonstrators march to Twickenham prior to the match against South Africa. December 1969. Photographer not known

Twenty-two year-old Lionel 'Big Train' Conacher is considered a
rugby player without equal in Canada. He is boxing champion of Ontario,
a member of the Toronto Argonaut football team, plays baseball
for Toronto Hillcrest, lacrosse for Toronto Maitlands and hockey for
the Toronto Canoe Paddlers. Circa 1923. Photographer not known

Opposite: Johnstone 'Jock' Richardson, All Blacks vice-captain.
September 1924. Photographer not known

Ireland players are
congratulated by fans
after their victory against
England at Twickenham.
February 1948.

Players' wives and girlfriends watch Workington Town RLFC. November 1950. Photograph by Jack Esten

Opposite: Bill Kingdon, Cec Ryan and fans walk to Kirkhall Lane rugby ground, Leigh. December 1949. Photograph by John Chillingworth

The British Combined Services rugby team attend a Japanese tea ceremony in Tokyo. March 1957. Photographer not known

The All Blacks perform the Haka for Prime Minister Kishi Nobusuke of Japan. February 1958. Photographer not known

The All Blacks arrive
at Tilbury Dock, London.
September 1935.
Photographer not known

Pupils at Marling School, Stroud, play touch rugby during a heatwave.
August 1937. Photographer not known

Opposite: The British Rugby League team train on a beach in Brisbane.
June 1962. Photographer not known

Neil Fox – known as 'The Points Machine'– puts his feet up after Wakefield Trinity's Rugby League Challenge Cup Final victory against Huddersfield. May 1962.
Photographer not known

Scots place their colours on the goal post
before the match against England at Twickenham.
March 1930. Photographer not known

Opposite: Scottish fans parade in the Mall before
travelling to Twickenham to see England play Scotland.
March 1934. Photographer not known

The Public School Wanderers prepare to set off on their tour of Devon and Cornwall. September 1951. Photographer not known

The Reading team arrive at Old Deer Park, Richmond, for their game against Rosslyn Park. September 1940. Photographer not known

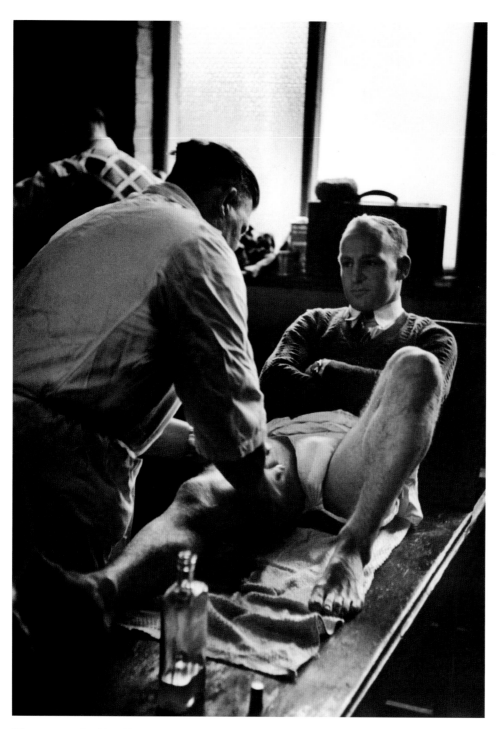

Wigan captain, New Zealander Cec Mountford, before the match against Warrington. December 1950. Photograph by Charles Hewitt

Opposite: Australian Arthur Clues watches his Leeds RLFC team-mate, New Zealander Bert Cook, enjoy a pedicure in the Scholl shop in the Queen's Arcade, Leeds. February 1949. Photograph by Haywood Magee

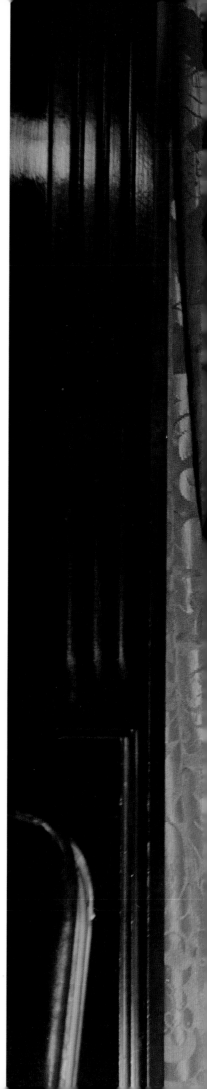

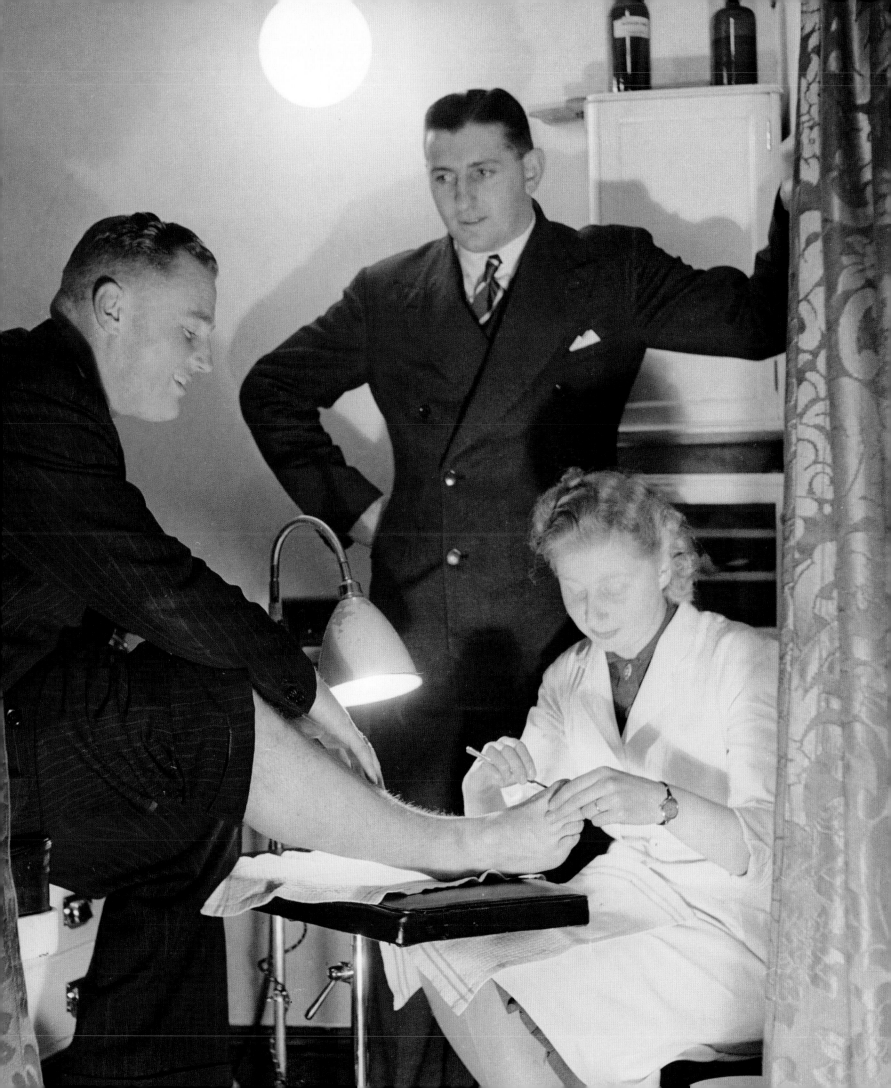

Opera singer Florence Austral fries eggs, sent by supporters, for the Australian Rugby League team at the Marlborough Hydro, Ilkley, Yorkshire. October 1933. Photographer not known

Opposite: The New South Wales Waratahs visit Jameson's distillery in Dublin. 1927. Photographer not known

Bridgewater players floodlit training.
November 1952. Photograph by Michael McKeown

Opposite: Cardiff Athletic practice session.
March 1949. Photograph by Joe Pazen

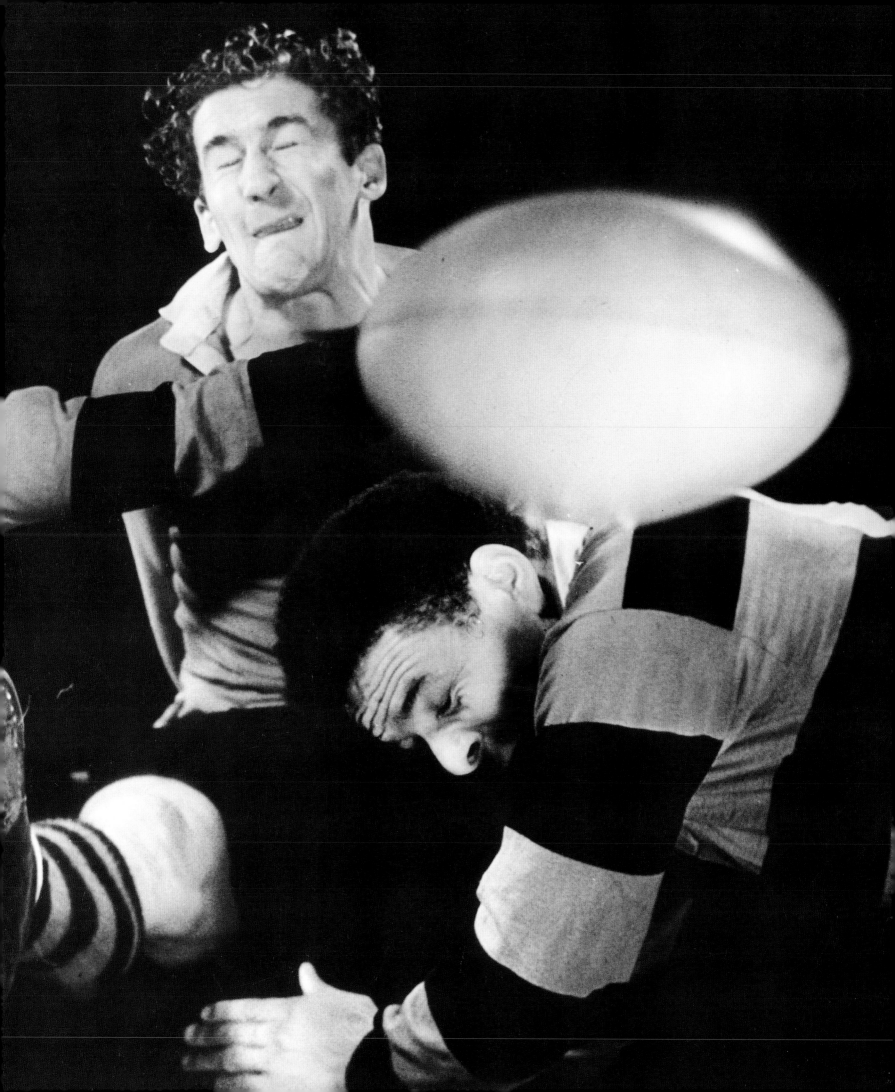

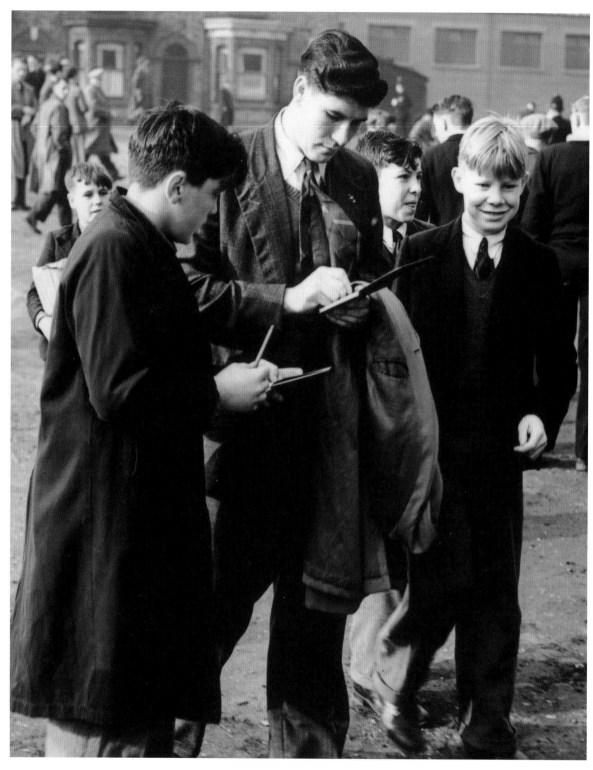

Wigan three-quarter Jack Broome with supporters. October 1950. Photograph by William Vanderson
Opposite: Wigan half-back Johnny Alty. October 1950. Photograph by William Vanderson

Leeds play Wakefield Trinity in the Rugby League Cup Final. May 1968. Photographer not known

Westminster Hospital play St. Mary's in the Hospital Cup. February 1978. Photographer not known

The crowd at Twickenham for the England versus Ireland match observe a minute's silence for victims of the Munich air crash. February 1958. Photographer not known

Esher Rugby Club post-match tea. December 1952. Photograph by Peter Waugh

Members of the Australian Rugby League team at a dance in Ilkley, Yorkshire. October 1952. Photograph by J. Simmons

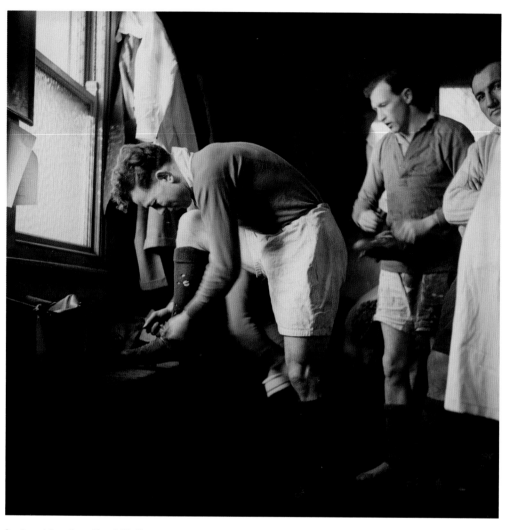

Ireland hooker Karl Mullen.
March 1951. Photograph by William Vanderson

Opposite: Bryn Evans and Trevor 'Tabber' Williams in the Welsh
dressing room at Cardiff Arms Park, after their match against Ireland.
March 1936. Photograph by Keating

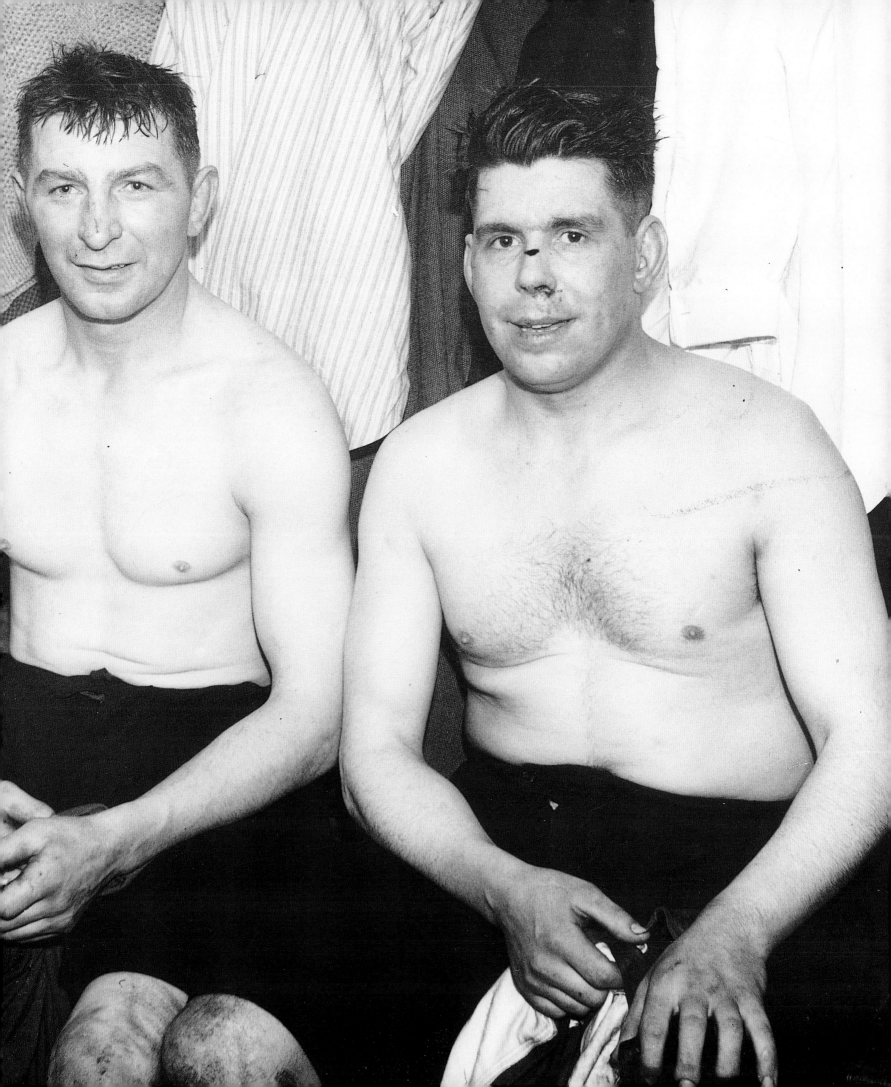

Sarah Ward and Cliff Morgan present 'Come Here Often' a twice-weekly
television programme for 9 to 14 year-olds. July 1967. Photographer not known

Opposite: Cliff Morgan runs out for Cardiff against Harlequins at Twickenham.
December 1955. Photographer not known

John Henry Collins played for Leigh RLFC in 1898 and now supervises the childrens' stand during matches. December 1949.
Photograph by John Chillingworth

Bath Rugby Club carries on, in spite of the destruction of the
stand and changing rooms in air raids during the Second World War.
December 1946. Photograph by Haywood Magee

Opposite: Bath Rugby Club players use the Roman baths as temporary
changing rooms. December 1946. Photograph by Haywood Magee

Sale Rugby Club training. December 1937. Photographer not known

Esher Rugby Club training. September 1949. Photograph by William Vanderson

Paddy Douglas, the Widnes RLFC captain, holds the Rugby League Challenge Cup at Euston station as the team prepare to return home. May 1930. Photographer not known

Guy's Hospital supporters before the match against Bart's. February 1931. Photograph by A. Hudson

Opposite: Before the Hospital Challenge Cup Final. March 1968. Photograph by Douglas Miller

Bath versus Bridgewater.
October 1946.
Photograph by Haywood Magee

Workington Town R.L.F.C.

Northern Rugby League

BORDER PARK - WORKINGTON

WORKINGTON TOWN
versus
LEEDS

CLOSED

LANCS. CUP
SOLD OUT — FINAL —
AT
SWINTON : NOV. 4TH
GROUND
TICKETS
2/6
ON SALE
(One ticket only per person)

Wigan play Warrington in the Lancashire Cup Final. November 1950. Photograph by Charles Hewitt

Opposite: Workington shops close for the big match. November 1950. Photograph by Jack Esten

Wales versus England at Cardiff Arms Park.
January 1938. Photographer not known

Jeffrey Burton, son of the Rosslyn Park Colts secretary. March 1941. Photographer not known

Doreen Stephenson presents a red rose to Salford captain Gus Risman. April 1939. Photographer not known

Unidentified rugby boots. 1950's.
Photograph by Charles Hewitt

Football kickabout under rugby posts at Purley Way, Croydon. January 1969. Photographer not known

Opposite: The 'Gary Owen' Gaelic Football Club practise on the Wormwood Scrubs playing field. October 1967. Photographer not known

Preceding page: Twickenham. February 1930. Photographer not known

Above and opposite: Hastings & Bexhill players enjoy their annual trip to play Dieppe. May 1953. Photograph by Bert Hardy

Anti-apartheid demonstrators before Swansea play South Africa. November 1969. Photographer not known

Opposite: Anti-apartheid demonstration before Victoria play South Africa at Melbourne Olympic Park. July 1971. Photographer not known

England players leave the field at Crystal Palace after the match against 'The Originals', the first full New Zealand team. The crowd laughed when the Haka was performed before the game and England were beaten 15–0. December 1905.
Photographer not known

Comedian Arthur Askey leads out a womens' rugby team before a charity game. Circa 1935. Photographer not known

Opposite: Oliver Reed with Australian tourists Garrick Fay and Stuart Gregory. November 1973. Photograph by Arthur Jones

Unidentified womens' rugby team. November 1969. Photograph by Ian Tyas

Fashion model Robina Lake with Catford Bridge players. January 1964. Photographer not known

Above and opposite: John 'Jack' Gregory before and after his first game for
Blackheath, having completed a twelve-month ban from the RFU for playing professionally
for Huddersfield RLFC. October 1948. Photographs by Charles Hewitt

All Blacks players during their stay at Newton Abbot, Devon. September 1935. Photograph by William Vanderson

Players from the New Zealand Maori rugby team during their visit to London. October 1926. Photograph by Macgregor

Welsh supporters celebrate their victory against England at Twickenham. January 1952. Photographer not known

Opposite: Crowd at Twickenham. December 1930. Photographer not known

W.E. Henley holds the Hospital Rugby Cup
after St Mary's victory over King's College Hospital.
March 1935. Photographer not known

Frik du Preez. March 1971. Photographer not known

Opposite: Bill Beaumont. January 1982. Photographer not known

Above and opposite: Designed by Kenneth Dalgliesh, the new weather vane at Twickenham depicts Hermes, messenger of the Gods, passing a ball to a rugby player. January 1950. Photographer not known

Jack Goodall's Halifax team-mates watch as he climbs Calf Rock on Ilkley Moor as they prepare for their forthcoming Rugby League Cup Final against Salford. May 1939. Photographer not known

Opposite: The Kiwis visit Ilkley Moor during the New Zealand Rugby League tour of England and France. September 1947. Photographer not known

Scotland captain Jim Telfer watches England captain Budge Rogers make the toss in the tunnel at Twickenham. March 1969.

Opposite: Budge Rogers will be England captain due to Dick Greenwood's injury playing squash. February 1969.

Eddie Waring, BBC Rugby League commentator. February 1969. Photograph by Ray Green

Opposite: Eddie Waring with members of the Australian Rugby League team at Keighley, where he will commentate on their forthcoming Test Match. October 1952. Photograph by J. Simmons

Wales centre John Dawes receives attention from trainer Gerry Lewis during the match against Ireland at Cardiff Arms Park. March 1965. Photograph by Martin Gilfeather

Cambridge University rugby team leave London for their tour of the United States. March 1934. Photograph by J.A. Hampton

The All Black 'Invincibles' leave London for Paris. January 1925. Photographer not known

Members of the rugby team at Malais Hall School in Yorkshire dig the ground bordering the pitch to grow vegetables for the war effort. April 1942.
Photographer not known

British Lions captain Carl Aarvold.
Circa 1930. Photographer not known

Opposite: Prince Alexander Obolensky throws in for Middlesex.
October 1938. Photographer not known

Spectators at Pontypridd watch Wales play England.
November 1936. Photographer not known

Nebby Cleworth (left), a labourer by trade, plays for Leigh RLFC
at the weekend. December 1949. Photograph by John Chillingworth

Opposite: Geoff Burke chats with a Leigh RLFC supporter.
December 1949. Photograph by John Chillingworth

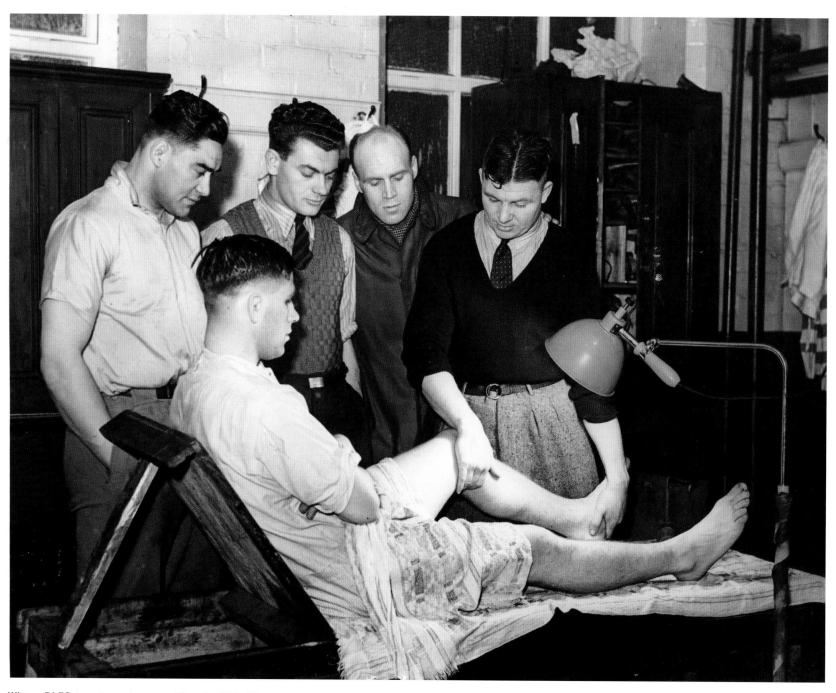

Wigan RLFC treatment room. March 1936. Photograph by Ward

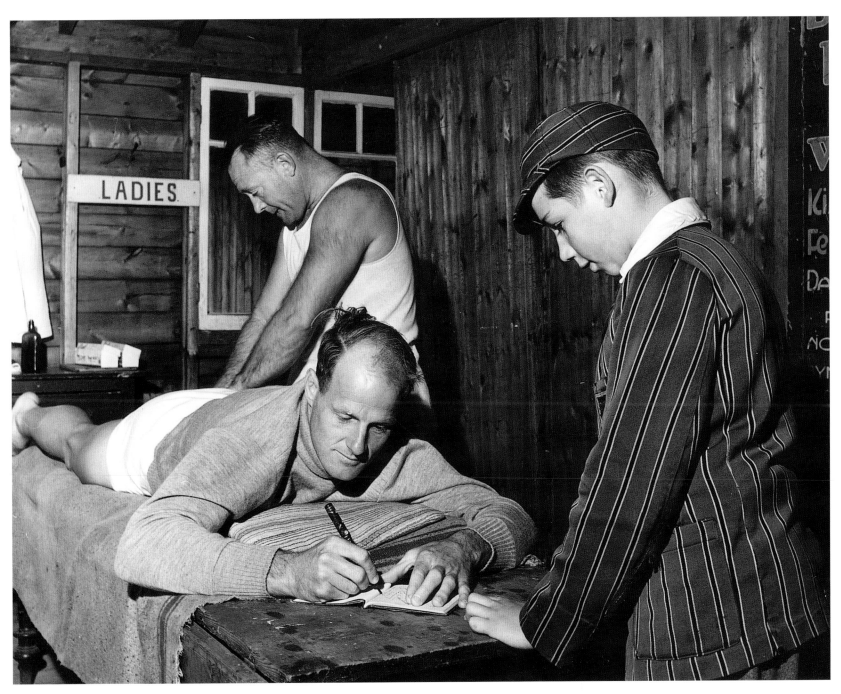

Noel Hazzard of the Australian Rugby League team. October 1952. Photograph by J. Simmons

Miners at Harworth Colliery,
Nottinghamshire, strike for
union recognition. April 1937.
Photograph by White

LET YOUR GOAL BE
CANADA FOR HOLIDAYS
BY
CANADIAN
PACIFIC

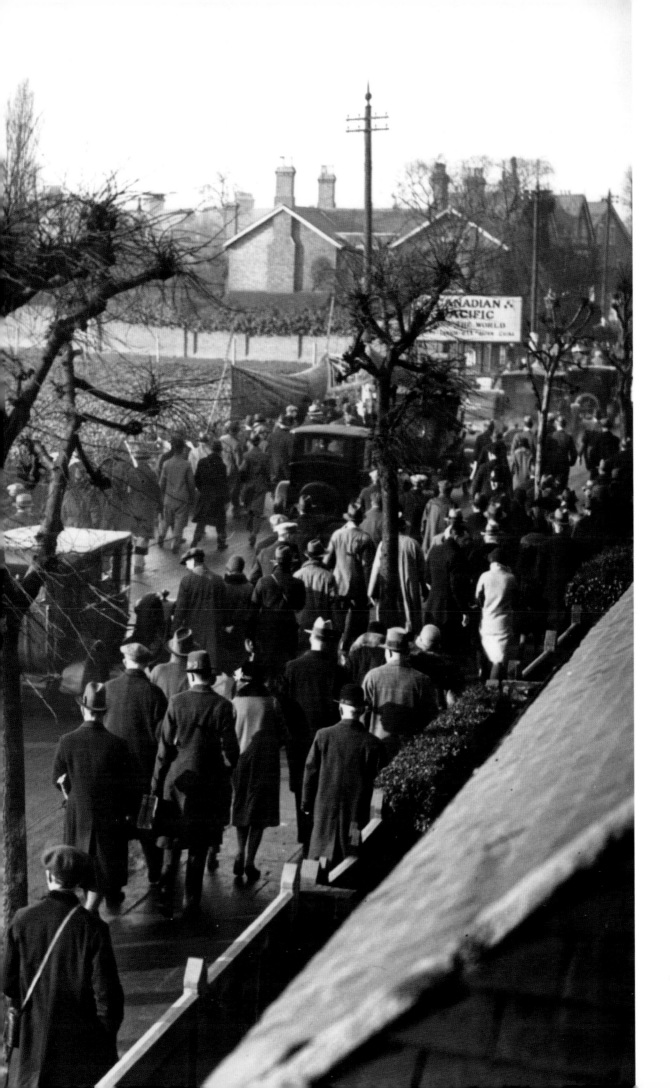

The road to Twickenham
before England play Wales.
January 1929.
Photographer not known

The London Society of Rugby Referees discuss the best position to assume during a scrum. September 1949. Photograph by R. Palmer

Dr. H.G. Owen Smith, the England full-back, demonstrates technique to Hornsey YMCA rugby team. November 1936. Photographer not known

Ireland forward, James Murphy-O'Connor during the match against England at Twickenham. February 1954. Photographer not known

Opposite: Wales lock, Don Hayward during the match against England at Twickenham. January 1950. Photographer not known

'Le Rugby' ballet by Susan Salaman. December 1930.
Photograph by Sasha

Terry Price of Llanelli and Wales. July 1967. Photograph by Don Morley

Opposite: Welsh scrum-half Gareth Edwards training in Sydney. July 1969. Photographer not known

Wigan RLFC half-back, Tommy Bradshaw (right) enjoys basket-making in his spare time. December 1950. Photograph by Charles Hewitt

Opposite: Scotland back-row forward, Doug Elliot is a sheep farmer in the border country. February 1949. Photographer not known

England train at St George's College, Weybridge. January 1964. Photographer not known

Opposite: British Lions captain Robin Thompson trains at Chelmsford Hall School, Eastbourne. June 1955. Photographer not known

Construction work at
Parc des Princes.
September 1971.

The Australian Rugby League team tour bus.
October 1952. Photograph by J. Simmons

Opposite: Unknown Australian Rugby League
player relaxes before the Test Match against England.
October 1952. Photograph by W.G. Vanderson

Retired miner and former rugby player for Workington RLFC, George Plummer relives past glories. November 1950. Photograph by Jack Esten
Opposite: Welsh painter Andrew Vicari in front of his portrait of Wales full-back Terry Davies. December 1960. Photograph by Chris Ware

England practice on the
Honourable Artillery Company's
pitch in London. January 1933.
Photographer not known

211

Leigh RLFC discuss tactics. December 1949. Photograph by John Chillingworth

Former Welsh international Garwyn Williams is now Rugby Coach at Whitgift School, Croydon. February 1955.

George Nepia, All Black full-back.
August 1924. Photograph by E. Bacon

Opposite: George Nepia arrives at Tilbury, after sailing
from New Zealand on the liner Akaroa. He is due to play his
first game for Streatham & Mitcham RLFC on Saturday.
December 1935. Photographer not known

Roofing work on the East Stand at Twickenham. July 1971. Photograph by Owen Lawrence

Opposite: The West Stand at Twickenham. Circa 1959. Photographer not known

Rival supporters watch Wales
play England at Llanelli. November 1938.
Photographer not known

Bath Rugby Club committee member Cyril Bailey addresses the bar. December 1946. Photograph by Haywood Magee

Courage Brewery director R. Quarry, RFU President A.G. Butler, Harlequins third team captain George Coppen and RFU secretary R. Prescott toast the opening of The Rugby Tavern at Twickenham. July 1963. Photographer not known

Australian Rugby League captain Reg Gasnier signs the ball used
in the Headingley Test for competition winner 15-year-old Keith Jones.
November 1967. Photographer not known

Opposite: 10-year-old Charles Sabourin joins in a Wallabies practice session
at Eastbourne College. October 1957. Photographer not known

West car park, Twickenham.
Circa 1927. Photographer not known

225

Jim Sullivan, Wigan RLFC trainer-coach, is the only man who can
kick a ball against the middle of the crossbar and catch it on the rebound.
December 1950. Photograph by Charles Hewitt

Opposite: Wigan team coaching session led by Jim Sullivan.
December 1950. Photograph by Charles Hewitt

Wellington, New Zealand. Circa 1930s.
Photograph by William Hall Raine

Former South African
cricketer H.G. Owen–Smith
coaches the England Rugby
Union team. January 1937.
Photographer not known

Barts supporters adopt a water can as their mascot for the Hospitals Rugby Cup Final against Kings College. March 1924. Photographer not known

Opposite: Barts supporter covered in flour, soot and red dye at the Hospitals Rugby Cup Final against Guys. March 1970. Photographer not known

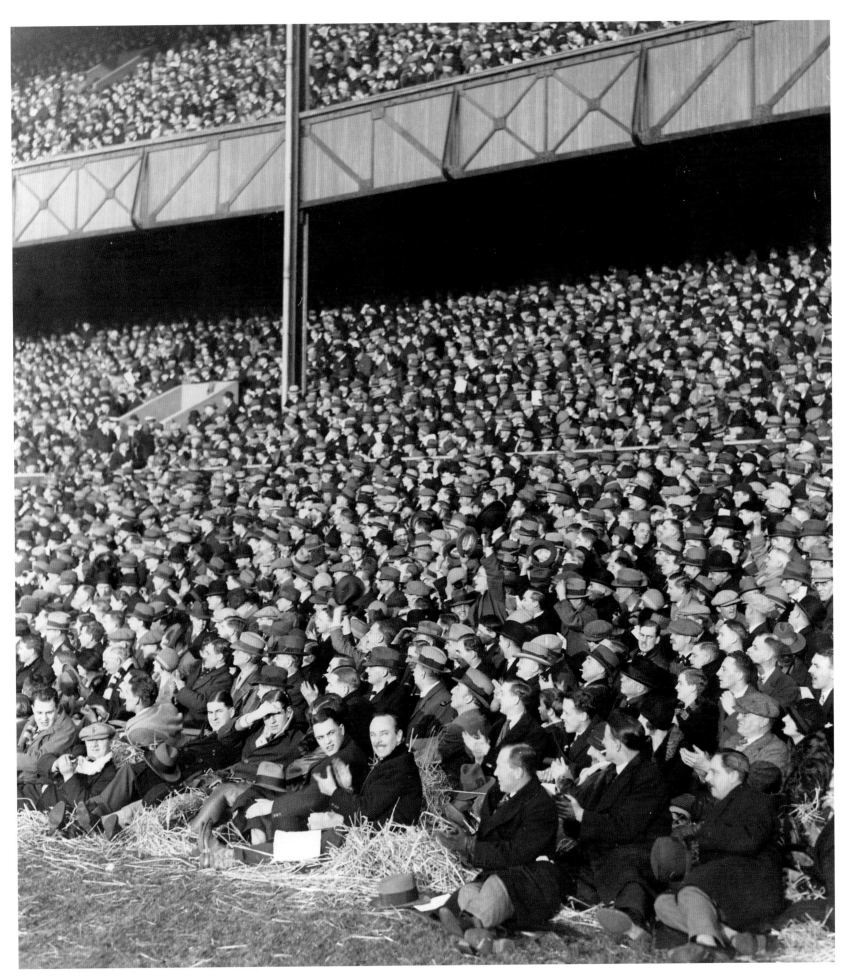

England versus Wales at Twickenham. January 1929. Photographer not known

Opposite: Queuing at Twickenham to see England play Wales. January 1937. Photographer not known

Esher Rugby Club bath.
December 1952. Photograph by Peter Waugh

Opposite: Australian Rugby League team bath.
October 1952. Photograph by William Vanderson

Murrayfield. April 1961.
Photographer not known

Fans in London for the Rugby League Cup Final between Huddersfield and Warrington. May 1933. Photographer not known

Fans in London for the Rugby League Cup Final between Leeds and Warrington. April 1936. Photographer not known

Fran Cotton, Peter Wheeler and Barry Nelmes at an England training session.
March 1978. Photographer not known

Opposite: John Dawes is chaired by Welsh team-mates as they celebrate
their victory in the Five Nations Tournament after beating France at Colombes.
March 1971. Photographer not known

Half-time in the
Oxford versus
Cambridge match
at Twickenham.
December 1930.

The Mayor of Southgate kicks off the charity match between Saracens and Trojans. January 1936. Photograph by David Savill
Opposite: Italian actress Milly Vitale kicks off the friendly between Blackheath and Milan. November 1957. Photographer not known

Vice Chairman of the Rugby League Mr A.A. Bonner, Secretary of the League Mr J. Wilson and Managing Director of Wembley Stadium Mr A. Elvin inspect turf to be laid for the Cup Final between Leeds and Warrington. March 1936. Photographer not known

Sam Goodman and Charlie Austin of the United States Olympic rugby team inspect the pitch before their first training session in England. April 1924. Photograph by Gill

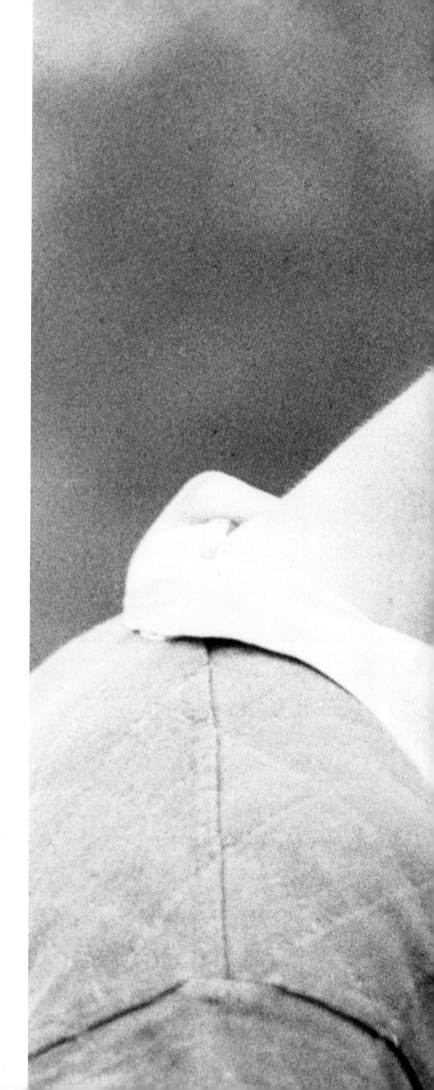

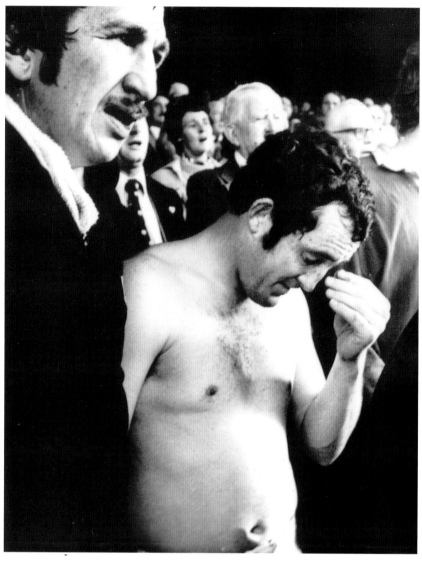

British Lions captain Phil Bennett after the fourth Test in Auckland. July 1977. Photographer not known

Opposite: All Blacks captain Brian Lochore after a training session during their European tour. October 1967. Photograph by Bob Aylott

Leeds versus Acton & Willesden at Park Royal.
April 1936. Photograph by J.A. Hampton

Welsh supporters before leaving Cardiff station for the match against Scotland at Murrayfield. January 1936. Photographer not known

Opposite: Welsh supporter in London. January 1937. Photographer not known

The New Zealand Maori team in Vancouver before
returning home after their 1926 tour of France,
England, Wales and Canada. Photographer not known

The Metropolitan Police and Paris Police teams before their
match in Paris. April 1947. Photographer not known

Opposite: A French mascot is removed from
the pitch at Twickenham before England play France.
February 1963. Photographer not known

Groundsmen at Twickenham protect the pitch from freezing. February 1958. Photographer not known

Sixty braziers are placed on the pitch at Cardiff Arms Park to help prevent it freezing. February 1956. Photographer not known

The Australian Rugby League team play Keighley at Lawkholme Lane. September 1952. Photograph by J. Simmons

Maine Road ground staff prepare for the Rugby League Cup Final between Salford and Castleford. May 1939. Photographer not known

Opposite: Leeds RLFC with the groundsmen at Wembley Stadium. April 1936. Photograph by J.A. Hampton

The game between London
Welsh and Newport is so
badly affected by fog
that spectators are allowed
to watch free of charge.
November 1950.
Photographer not known

The Reiley brothers play for London Irish. February 1937. Photograph by Douglas Miller

The Cogbill brothers play for Llanharen Rugby Club. December 1935. Photographer not known

Willie John McBride leads out Ireland at Twickenham. February 1974. Photographer not known

Opposite: Fran Cotton runs out at Twickenham. January 1977. Photographer not known

Edinburgh University Women's rugby team.
May 1962. Photograph by Loomis Dean

Opposite: Edinburgh University Women's rugby
team relax after a match.
May 1962. Photograph by Loomis Dean

Filming the caption close-up prior to the game. January 1955. Photographer not known

Peter West and Wilf Wooller commentate on the match between England and Wales. January 1955. Photographer not known

Australians from the 59th Battalion play
behind the lines on the Somme.
September 1918. Photographer not known

Esher Rugby Club secretary Aubrey Downey explains the game to visiting American soldiers. December 1952. Photograph by Peter Waugh

Opposite: Unknown rugby club in the United States. January 1939. Photograph by Wallace Kirkland

JPR Williams is tackled by England's Malcolm Young.
February 1978. Photographer not known

Opposite: JPR Williams breaks his cheekbone tackling Scotland's Billy Steele.
February 1972. Photographer not known

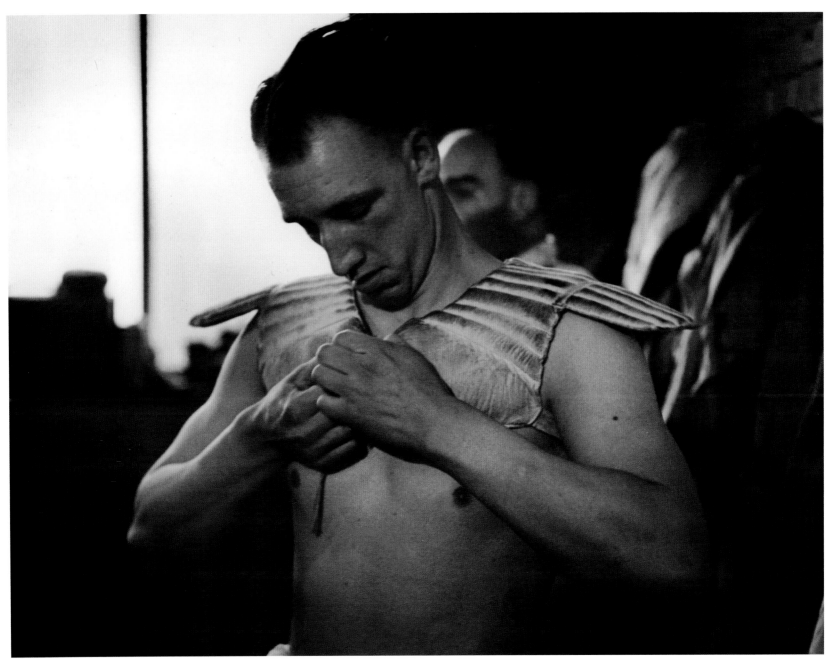

Above and opposite: Wigan hooker Ronnie Mather padding-up before the game against Warrington.
December 1950. Photographs by Charles Hewitt

England versus New Zealand Rugby League Test Match. Circa 1960. Photographer not known

Opposite: Australia versus England Rugby League Test Match. June 1950. Photographer not known

England practice session.
January 1933. Photographer not known

Opposite: Springboks captain Paul Roos holds the ball
while Dougie 'Zulu' Morkel practises his kicking
during the 1906 European tour. Photographer not known

Unknown Australian women's match. October 1930. Photographer not known

Opposite: Worthing Rugby Club organise a match against their female supporters. February 1966. Photographer not known

Rochdale Hornets RLFC mid-week game.
April 1952. Photograph by Jack Esten

England at half-time during their match against Wales at St Helen's, Swansea. January 1924. Photographer not known

Half-time during Wales versus Scotland at Cardiff Arms Park. February 1927. Photograph by Kirby

Courtenay Meredith, Robin Thompson and D.S. 'Tug' Wilson train at
Chelmsford Hall School, Eastbourne before the British Lions tour of South Africa.
June 1955. Photographer not known

Opposite: British Lion Angus Cameron at Chelmsford Hall School.
June 1955. Photographer not known

Harlequins player, the Reverend W.S. Kemble, curate of St. Matthews in Bethnal Green, coaching local boys.
October 1938. Photographer not known

Stella Baker, warden of the Rodney Youth Centre, plays scrum-half in the ballroom of the Wellington Rooms in Liverpool.
March 1949. Photograph by Charles Hewitt

Assistant rink manager
Joe Durling coaches ice
rugby for Streatham
Juniors ice hockey team.
July 1950.
Photographer not known

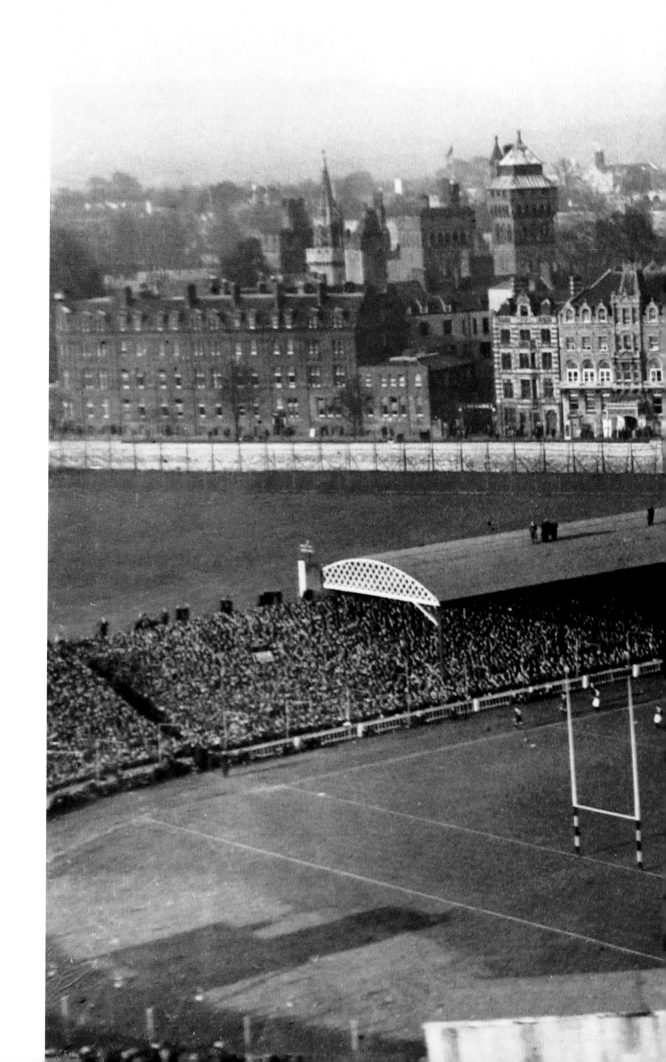

Cardiff Arms Park. March 1932.
Photographer not known

Warrington beat Widnes in the Rugby League Cup Final at Wembley. May 1950. Photographer not known

Opposite: Wigan beat Barrow in the Rugby League Cup Final at Wembley. May 1951. Photographer not known

The British Isles Rugby team, with their mascot Felix, at Waterloo Station before their tour of South Africa. June 1924. Photograph by E. Bacon

The British Lions at Waterloo Station before their tour of Australia and New Zealand. April 1930. Photographer not known

England versus Australia at Twickenham. February 1958. Photographer not known

Opposite: Oxford University rugby trials. October 1950. Photograph by John Chillingworth

306

The Bacon School,
Bermondsey. March 1955.
Photographer not known

Harry Varley of England and Liversedge RFC. Circa 1896. Photographer not known

Opposite: W. McCutcheon of Wales and Oldham RFC. Circa 1891. Photographer not known

Wigan RLFC captain Cec Mountford with his wife, Edna, and daughter, Carolyn. December 1950. Photograph by Charles Hewitt
Opposite: Former Leigh RLFC player Bob Montford arrives home after work. December 1949. Photograph by John Chillingworth

Huddersfield play St. Helens in the Rugby League Cup Final at Wembley. April 1953. Photographer not known

Rugby League International between Wales and Australia. January 1930. Photograph by Puttnam

University College supporters at the Inter-College Rugby Cup Final. April 1923. Photographer not known

Opposite: Guys and Barts supporters. Circa 1920. Photographer not known

Peter, the Warrington RLFC mascot, heads the ball to his team-mates during a training session.
March 1936. Photographer not known

Opposite: Salford RLFC train on the beach at Blackpool in preparation for the Rugby League Cup Final against Castleford.
May 1939. Photographer not known

Wigan RLFC supporters.
January 1968.
Photograph by Ray Green

Leighton Buzzard and Harrow Schools introduce mechanical tackling devices for rugby practice. October 1943. Photographer not known

Lancing House School, Lowestoft. October 1934. Photograph by Martin

**England players after beating Wales
at St Helens in Swansea. January 1924.**
Photographer not known

Mike Campbell-Lamerton and Peter Stagg during a Scotland training session. January 1965. Photographer not known

Opposite: Perse linesman A.J. Brylewski. April 1963. Photographer not known

Olympic 100-yards bronze medallist, Emmanuel McDonald Bailey signs for Leigh RLFC. December 1953. Photographer not known

Opposite: Oxford University's John Coker, the first black African to win a Blue. December 1965. Photographer not known

The Artists Rifles rugby team after their match against The Public Schools rugby team. December 1915. Photographer not known

The Public Schools rugby team. December 1915. Photographer not known

Cardiff Arms Park. February 1935. Photographer not known

French supporters on the pitch at Twickenham. February 1959. Photographer not known

Opposite: French supporters on the pitch at Twickenham. February 1969. Photographer not known

The crowd at Oldham versus Rochdale Hornets.
November 1954. Photograph by Bert Hardy

Pupils of County School, Harrow, are coached by Mr Bomford and Mr Venn.
March 1952. Photographer not known

A ball is lost when West Ham Secondary School play The Baines Foundation at Leytonstone Rugby Ground.
December 1959. Photographer not known

Leeds RLFC captain Jim Brough after beating Warrington in the Rugby League Cup Final at Wembley. He shows the cup to the Leeds schoolboys, brought to the match by special train. April 1936.

The New Zealand Rugby League team, The Kiwis, perform the Haka before their Test Match against England at Central Park, Wigan. October 1926. Photographer not known

Opposite: The All Blacks perform the Haka at Lansdowne Road. January 1954. Photograph by Charles Hewitt

Police constables
John Atkinson of Leeds
RLFC and Trevor Briggs
of Dewsbury RLFC.
October 1977.
Photograph by John Varley

Lancashire wing three-quarter C.B. Holmes practises for the match against Durham. November 1938. Photographer not known

Swinton RLFC passing practice is supervised by Mr Kershaw. November 1937. Photographer not known

Wales versus England at Cardiff Arms Park.
January 1922. Photographer not known

The Springboks return home after their British tour. February 1952. Photograph by J.A. Hampton

Opposite: British Lions captain Ronnie Cove-Smith with Captain Strong of the 'Edinburgh Castle', as the team sail to South Africa. June 1924. Photograph by E. Bacon

Wavell Wakefield before his last game for
England, against France at Stade Colombes in Paris.
April 1927. Photographer not known

The French team at Victoria Station. February 1928. Photographer not known

The Argentinian team in London. January 1963. Photographer not known

Impromptu schoolboy game during half-time at Twickenham. April 1955. Photographer not known

The England Rugby League team travel to Australia on board 'HMS Indomitable'. April 1946. Photograph by Bush
Opposite: Royal Australian Air Force fighter station in the Western Desert. November 1942. Photographer not known

Springbok captain Avril Malan on board the
'Pretoria Castle' as the team arrive at Southampton.
October 1960. Photographer not known

Opposite: Councillor Edward Woodward-Cross,
Mayor of Southampton, greets the Springbok touring team.
September 1931. Photographer not known

Harrow School pupil. Circa 1935. Photographer not known

Opposite: Leicester & Midland Counties player C. Slow owns a shoe shop in Northampton. November 1931. Photographer not known

England training session at St George's College,
Weybridge. February 1964. Photographer not known

Jack Cunliffe, playing for Great Britain Tourists, fails to prevent Brian Bevan scoring for The Best of The League at Central Park, Wigan. October 1950.
Photographer not known

England versus Ireland at
Twickenham. Previously postponed,
following the death of King George VI,
the match is played a month later
in a blizzard. March 1952.
Photographer not known

Spectators watch Coventry versus Harlequins. November 1949. Photograph by Auerbach

Opposite: England forward David Powell during the match against Ireland at Twickenham. February 1966. Photographer not known

Widnes RLFC practise
for their Rugby League
Cup Final against
Keighley. May 1937.

36-24-36 Club versus Medway Brigands RFC charity match.
January 1967. Photographer not known

Opposite: After the London University Men versus Women student match.
March 1963. Photographer not known

Twickenham. June 1935.
Photographer not known

Rugby School, Warwickshire.
October 1923. Photographer not known

INDEX

PHOTOGRAPHIC CREDITS

ACKNOWLEDGEMENTS

For George Benjamin Goater.

My special thanks to:
Howard Evans, Robert Gate, Julie Tennant and Robin Douglas-Withers
for perfect line-out calls throughout this project.

Thanks also to the following people for their patience, support and expertise:

Alan Ashby, Paul Beken, Kate Belcher, Jonathan Bloom, Gordon Burn, Julia Carmichael,
Martin Creasey, Nick Culpeper, Lucy Davey, Madelaine Debnam, Mark Debnam,
Coralie Dorman, Matthew Drennan, Morag Farquhar, Jeff Foreman, Dorothy Frame,
Alison Gardiner, Alice Goater, Nick Goater, David Godwin, Seamus Geoghegan, Carol Gorner,
Ken Griffiths, Steve Guise, Brendan Hayes, Deborah Hayes, Shem Law, Lindsay Marriott,
Oliver Maxey, David Middleton, Keith Mills, Peter Murray, Tony Phillips, Les Pipe,
Michael Potter, Christina Quaine, Stephen Rabson, Gillian Rhys, David Robson, Tommy Sale,
Jo Sandilands, Andy Saunders, Peter Campbell Saunders, Sarah Savitt, Tom Shone,
Julie Stevens, Sally Taylor, Jack Tennant, John Varley, JPR Williams, Mitzie Wilson
and my Mum & Dad.

From Cassell Illustrated:

Anna Cheifetz, Liz Fowler, Auberon Hedgecoe, Gabrielle Mander, Adam Smith and Jen Veall.

From picture sources:

Nicole Newman at Corbis.
Martin Aspley, Graham Atkinson, Emily Lewis and Neil Simpson at EMPICS.
Bob Ahern, Liz Ihre, Charles Merullo, Sarah Parkinson and Teresa Riley at Getty Images.
Ian Blackwell and Vito Inglese at Popperfoto.
Gayle Mault, Venita Paul and Chris Rowling at Science & Society Picture Library.
Jed Smith at the Museum of Rugby, Twickenham.
Mark Dowd at Topfoto.
Tim Corballis at The Alexander Turnbull Library, New Zealand.

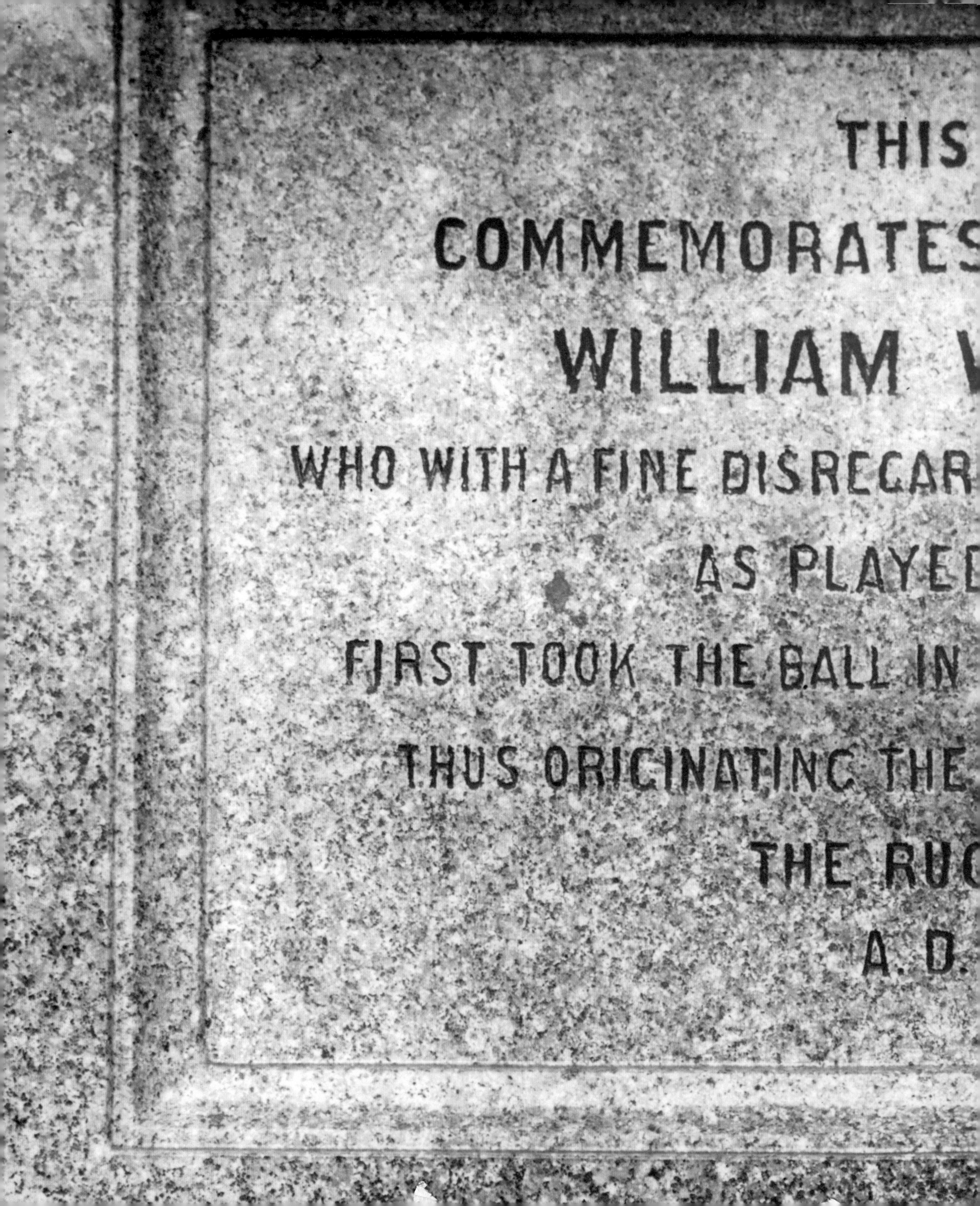

THIS

COMMEMORATES

WILLIAM W

WHO WITH A FINE DISREGAR

AS PLAYED

FIRST TOOK THE BALL IN

THUS ORIGINATING THE

THE RUG

A. D